U0099995

李浩然 + 尹國華（基本法基金會）

國籍的抉擇

香港
永久性居民
身份研究

三聯書店網址：
www.jointpublishing.com

Facebook 搜尋：
三聯書店 Joint Publishing

WeChat 帳號：
jointpublishinghk

責任編輯	培　中
書籍設計	金小曼
插　　圖	溫　溫

書　　名	國籍的抉擇——香港永久性居民身份研究
著　　者	李浩然　尹國華
出　　版	三聯書店（香港）有限公司
	香港北角英皇道 499 號北角工業大廈 20 樓
	Joint Publishing (H.K.) Co., Ltd.
	20/F., North Point Industrial Building,
	499 King's Road, North Point, Hong Kong
香港發行	香港聯合書刊物流有限公司
	香港新界荃灣德士古道 220-248 號 16 樓
印　　刷	美雅印刷製本有限公司
	香港九龍觀塘榮業街 6 號 4 樓 A 座
版　　次	2021 年 1 月香港第一版第一次印刷
	2024 年 6 月香港第一版第二次印刷
規　　格	32 開（125 mm × 176 mm）96 面
國際書號	ISBN 978-962-04-4777-8

前言

　　香港社會在回歸前曾出現過一陣海外移民潮，當時不少中產階層皆因為政治前景不明朗等原因，選擇舉家移居海外，也有先安排子女前往外地求學並由部分家人陪同在海外照顧，而主要賺錢養家的則繼續留在香港謀生。當年亦廣泛報導過，這些分隔兩地的移民家庭曾發生不少問題。除了婚姻出現危機甚至破裂外，也有不少因為不適應而回流的個案，導致一連串就業和住屋的社會問題。

　　再者，在回歸前英國政府還給予 5 萬個香港家庭居英權，雖然沒有相關研究統計，到底有多少以此配額移居英國的個案，但是一般相信選擇繼續在香港居留的那些擁有居英權的人士，基本上仍然保留了已取得的英國國籍[1]。另一方面，因應 2019 年的「反修例」事件引發的社會動亂而訂立的《香港特別行政區維護國家安全法》，在社會上又重燃新一浪移民潮的熱烈討論。

　　加上近日英國政府高調公佈，幫助香港人可以持 BNO 護照快捷獲取英國居留權，令相關討論與猜測甚囂塵上。本書試圖梳理回歸後移居海外香港居民身份的變化、居英權的影響以至 BNO 護照持有人的權利等問題，並作出深入探討和分析。

目 錄

附錄

I

關於
香港永久性居民
身份的研究

回歸前港府的出入境政策

香港政府在回歸前的出入境政策，對香港永久居民身份的要求是比較寬鬆的，只要有中國血統並在香港居住滿 7 年便被視為擁有香港永久性居民身份[2]，甚至連部分持有英國護照或是英聯邦地區的公民也得到同等待遇。當時的香港政府一直默許前文所述移居海外的香港人持有雙重身份，哪怕他們已經離開香港定居海外，以至拿到外國的國籍，他們仍可以繼續保留香港永久性居民身份，隨意回流香港並工作，兼且繼續享有移民前的福利和待遇。

然而，在回歸後香港特別行政區依照《基本法》的規定進行管治，如此香港永久性居民的身份，亦應該由《基本法》第 24 條所釐定。因此，特區政府現行政策應否仍保持在回歸前的思維？還是應該主動切實履行其憲制責任，從實體法律和行政政策上充分體現《基本法》第 24 條的立法意圖和精神？其答案是不言而喻的。

《基本法》第 24 條的規定

根據《基本法》第 24 條的規定，香港特別行政區永久性居民包括如下類別人士：

（一）在香港出生的中國公民（要件一：香港出生；要件二：中國公民）；

（二）在香港通常居住連續 7 年以上的中國公民（要件一：在香港連續居住 7 年；要件二：中國公民）；

（三）（一）或者（二）居民在香港以外所生的中國籍子女〔要件一：（一）或者（二）項所指人士；要件二：其子女在外地出生；要件三：擁有中國籍〕；

（四）持有效旅遊證件進入香港、在香港通常居住連續 7 年以上，並以香港作為永久居住地的非中國籍人士（要件一：外籍人士；要件二：在香港合法地連續居住 7 年；要件三：以香港作為永久居住地，即必須主觀上有決心、客觀上有安排和能力永久居住在香港）；

（五）（四）項居民在香港所生的未滿 21 周歲的子女；〔要件一：（四）項所指的人士；要件二：子女在香港出生；要件三：不足 21 周歲〕；

（六）（一）至（五）項所列居民以外，在特區成立前只在香港有居留權人士（並不符合前五項人士，仍可以此條件獲取）。

根據經驗所知，前文所述的在回歸前從香港移民海外人士，絕大部分皆是（一）和（二）項的類別。而作為這兩種類別的人士，他們的共同特點就是必須為「中國公民」。由此而引申的第一個需要探討的問題是，根據《中

圖一：《基本法》第 24 條對香港特區永久性居民的規定

（一）在香港出生的中國公民

（二）在香港通常居住連續 7 年以上
的中國公民

（三）（一）或者（二）項人士在
香港以外所生的中國籍子女

（四）持有效旅遊證件進入香港並在此通常居住連續 7 年以上，並以香港作為永久居住地的非中國籍人士。

（五）（四）項人士在港所生的未滿 21 歲子女

（六）（一）至（五）項以外，在特區成立前只在香港有居留權人士。

華人民共和國國籍法》(「《國籍法》」) 第三條規定:「中華人民共和國不承認中國國民具有雙重國籍。」如果這些移居海外並拿到外國國籍的香港人,或者打算移居海外的香港永久性居民,清楚了解到這個雙重國籍問題會令他們失去香港永久性居民身份,結果必然會一定程度地影響他們將會作出的決定或者安排,所以有必要從多角度去深入分析。

05 首先,從法庭案例考慮,雖然回歸後香港法院也曾審理過很多關於《基本法》第 24 條的案件,但是相關的爭議點主要圍繞在父母僅是中國公民而非香港永久性居民在香港出生的子女 [3],以及香港永久性居民在內地出生的子女 [4] 能否擁有香港永久居留權的問題上。雖然部分也涉及外籍人士在香港居住滿 7 年而產生的居留權爭議,其中包括何謂「通常居住地」[5]、「永久居住地」[6] 和「連續居住」[7] 等的定義;可是,對於國籍身份的改變會否導致香港永久性居民身份的喪失,卻沒有任何案例可以參考。

06 從《基本法》第 24 條的字面解釋,(一) 和 (二) 項其中一個重要焦點就是中國公民身份的要素。

中國公民身份的規定

07 根據《中華人民共和國憲法》第 33 條第一款規定:「凡具有中華人民共和國國籍的人都是中華人民共和國公

民。」因此，所有擁有中國國籍的人皆是中國公民。

　　作為《基本法》附件三內的全國性法律，《國籍法》在回歸後便在香港特別行政區公佈實施。相關的主要條文包括：

　　第三條　中華人民共和國不承認中國公民具有雙重國籍。

　　第四條　父母雙方或一方為中國公民，本人出生在中國，具有中國國籍。

　　第五條　父母雙方或一方為中國公民，本人出生在外國，具有中國國籍；但父母雙方或一方為中國公民並定居在外國，本人出生時即具有外國國籍的，不具有中國國籍。

　　第六條　父母無國籍或國籍不明，定居在中國，本人出生在中國，具有中國國籍。

　　第九條　定居外國的中國公民，自願加入或取得外國國籍的，即自動喪失中國國籍。

　　從《國籍法》第九條看，所有中國公民也擁有中國籍；如此類推，《基本法》第 24 條中的中國公民身份要素可以同樣被理解為需要擁有中國國籍的必要條件。

　　由始至終，香港一直被認定為是中國不可分割的一部分，所以，無論是在內地出生而後來移居香港的人，還是在香港土生土長的人，在《國籍法》下也應該被視為是

圖二：《中國國籍法》的國籍身份規定

第三條

不承認雙重國籍

母　　父

子女

第四條

父母雙方或一方為中國公民
在中國出生

母　父

子女

第五條

父母雙方或一方為中國公民
在外國出生，具有中國國籍；
或父母雙方或一方為中國公民並
定居在外國
在外國出生時即具有外國國籍，
不具有中國國籍。

母　父

子女

第六條

父母無國籍或國籍不明
定居中國在中國出生
具中國國籍

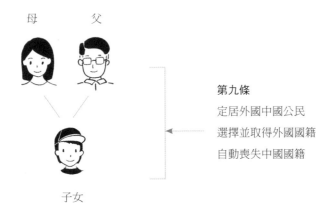

母　父

子女

第九條

定居外國中國公民

選擇並取得外國國籍

自動喪失中國國籍

在中國出生的。因此，只要父母一方是中國公民，依據《國籍法》第四條，這些在香港出生的人就會自動擁有中國國籍。然而，這分析還是擺脫不了一個迴環的概念，因為對於出生在內地或者香港的人，要確切判斷他們是否擁有中國國籍還需要從源頭追溯其父母、其父母的父母是否中國公民，如果答案是肯定的，他們才被納入《國籍法》第四條而擁有中國國籍。

11　　對於這個問題，按照 1996 年 5 月 15 日全國人大常委會第 19 次會議通過的《關於〈中華人民共和國國籍法〉在香港特別行政區實施的幾個問題的解釋》（「《解釋》」）第一段所闡述：「凡具有中國血統的香港居民，本人出生在中國領土（含香港）者，以及其他符合《中華人民共和國國籍法》規定的具有中國國籍的條件者，都是中國公民。」

12　　簡而言之，所有擁有中國血統的香港居民，無論是在內地出生還是在香港出生，他們不單只擁有中國國籍，而且還是中國公民。進一步來說，所有擁有中國血統並在香港出生的人也滿足《基本法》第 24 條（一）項的要求而擁有香港永久性居民身份。

13　　無論如何，香港永久性居民身份必須建立在中國公民的前提下。然而，另外一個需要考慮的衍生問題就是當失去了這個中國公民身份時，之前所得到的香港永久性居民身份是否會一併失去？換言之，依據《基本法》第 24

條（一）和（二）項而取得香港永久性居民身份的人，是否需要一直保持中國公民這個條件才能保留在香港的永久居留權？言下之意所謂的永久居留權不一定可以永久保留。

《基本法》第 24 條下的中國公民的必要條件

對於《基本法》第 24 條（一）項類別的香港永久性居民，絕大部分是擁有中國血統的人，這些人的祖輩就是在內地出生然後移居香港的中國人，當然也包括一些香港的原居民後裔。如果中國公民這個條件只是在出生時才考慮，出生後就不用維持，接受這解釋就必然得出一個奇怪的結論，中國公民這個條件在《基本法》第 24 條（一）項裡可以說是毫無意義的，幾乎是完全可以被取代的。因為根據前文《國籍法》的推論，這些人出生的時候就自動擁有中國籍而成為中國公民，在《基本法》第 24 條（一）項無需重複強調中國公民這要求。如果立法意圖是該永久性居民身份獲取後便永遠不會喪失的話，（一）項只需簡化表述為「在香港出生的具有中國血統的人」便足夠，因為血統是不變的事實，不像國籍般有機會改變，這樣也同時銜接了回歸前香港政府的入境政策。由此可以推論在《基本法》第 24 條裡「中國公民」的使用必然有更深層次的原因。就算從普通法法理的角度去分析，法律條文內所包含的每一字句也應該有其特定的意義和目的 [8]。因此，合理的推斷是這個條件必須持續滿足，否則香港永久居留權就隨著中國公民身份的消失而同時失去。當然，還有一種很不常見的情況，就是申請人雖然在香港出生，可是出生時並非中國公民，但後來卻根據《國籍法》歸化而取得中國國籍並成為中國公民，由此而同時取得香港永久性居民身份。然而這種理解也不會和維持中國公民身份作為需要持續滿足的條件產生任何衝突。

15   對於《基本法》第 24 條（一）、（二）項的規定，因為文理結構有類同的地方，亦可以借鑒於（五）項類別的規定。作為（四）項居民的子女，出生時也會自動成為香港永久性居民，然而，當他不能滿足「未滿 21 周歲」這必要條件時，他就自動失去香港永久居留權 [9]。當然，如果他在滿 21 周歲前能連續在香港居住 7 年，而且還以香港作為永久居住地，他就可以像他父母一樣依據（四）項規定而繼續擁有香港永久性居民身份。跟（一）項類同的地方是當申請人出生時，他可能還沒中國公民身份，但是這不影響當他取得相關身份後就滿足（一）項的要求；而跟（二）項的情況比較，申請人在香港出生時父母可能還沒有滿足（四）項的要求，但只要在他滿 21 周歲前他的父母能成為（四）項所指的人士，他就能根據（五）項而取得香港永久性居民身份 [10]。由此可以得出必要條件的改變，將影響獲取香港永久性居民身份的結論。

16　　　這個必須擁有中國公民身份以獲取香港永久居民身份的必要條件的立法意圖，也可以從《基本法》第 24 條（三）項的字面體現出來。哪怕父母雙方也是擁有中國血統的香港永久性居民，他們在外國出生的子女必須還是中國籍（即中國公民）才是香港永久性居民。

17　　　縱觀前述，中國公民身份在《基本法》第 24 條佔有重要的地位，它的取得會影響是否滿足相關條款的要求，從而影響是否滿足成為香港永久性居民的身份。同理，沒有任何理據支持這個條件只需要在申請時滿足就足夠，在得到永久性居民身份後便不用繼續保留。這種說法明顯忽略中國公民在《基本法》第 24 條內的重要性。因此，基於個人選擇或原因失去中國公民身份後，他的香港永久性居民身份也應同時喪失。

地域的聯繫或者國籍的聯繫

18　　　然而還需要補充一點，就是必須保留中國公民身份以保留香港永久性居民身份，只是針對於那些離開香港移居外地的人。對於繼續居住在香港的人，哪怕他因為獲取到別國的國籍而失去了中國公民身份，他也可以依據（四）項保留香港永久性居民的身份。當然，這種情況在現實中可能非常罕見，除了憑藉居英權而得到英國國籍的人士，他們有機會被認定為已經喪失中國公民身份。可

是，根據《國籍法》，中國國籍的自動喪失只會在定居國
外後並取得外國國籍才出現，所以，很大機會這些擁有居
英權的人士並沒有喪失中國國籍，因為其英國國籍不被承
認，除非當事人主動申請放棄中國國籍並且獲得批准。

19

　　由此可以看出《基本法》第 24 條是建立在兩個聯繫
上，一個就是地域的聯繫，即居住在香港；另外一個就是
身份的聯繫，即維持中國公民的身份，兩者的同時消失意
味著香港永久性居民地位的喪失。

20

　　擁有香港永久居留權而移居海外人士的身份變化，
可以如下分類：

移居時仍然是中國公民

　　（一）這些仍然是中國公民但決定移居海外的香
港永久性居民，在取得外國國籍前仍然保留中國公民
身份，所以仍擁有香港永久性居民的地位；但是當獲
得外國國籍後，根據《國籍法》第九條便會自動失去
中國公民身份，並應同時失去香港永久性居民地位，
自此以後，他們在國外出生的子女也不會得到香港永
久性居民身份。簡單而言，他們已經變成中國裔的外
籍人士，不能以中國公民身份繼續保持香港永久性居
民的地位，他們的子女也不可以依據《基本法》第 24
條（三）項而取得香港永久性居民身份。

　　（二）然而，當這些已經取得外國國籍的人回流
香港定居，他們在香港出生的子女，只要出生時沒有

其他國家的國籍（不能跟《國籍法》第三條衝突），雖然其父母已經是外籍人士，但事實上卻擁有中國血統，根據《解釋》就自動擁有中國國籍，從而根據《基本法》第 24 條（一）項而取得香港永久性居民身份。然而，如果他們的子女出生時自動擁有外國國籍，他們的子女也只能依據《基本法》第 24 條（四）或（五）項才可取得香港永久性居民身份。

（三）當這些移居人士仍然沒有取得外國國籍而繼續保留其中國公民身份時，其在外地出生的子女只要不擁有外國國籍，根據《國籍法》第五條，便自動擁有中國籍，所以在《基本法》第 24 條（三）項下仍然是香港永久性居民；但是只要出生時擁有外國國籍，或者往後定居在海外並取得外國國籍者，也會因《國籍法》第九條自動失去中國公民身份，至此也會同時喪失香港永久性居民身份。

移居時並非中國公民

（四）簡而言之，當正常獲得了其他國家國籍時，中國公民身份理應會同時喪失，這時候離開香港移居海外，可能會因為不符合《基本法》第 24 條（四）項的要求，即以香港作為永久居住地而失去永久居留權。然而從字面上理解，《國籍法》第九條只適用於由定居而取得的外國國籍，所以，非以此管道取得的

圖三：圖解香港人移居外地能否繼續擁有香港永久性居民身份

香港人移居外地並領取外國國籍，
原香港永久性居民身份便即時註銷。

香港人移居外地但仍保留中國國籍，
則可以繼續擁有香港永久性居民身份。

外國國籍身份有可能不被中國政府承認而仍然保留中國國籍，繼續享有中國公民的地位和香港永久性居民的待遇。

香港特區入境事務處的現行政策

21　　香港法例第 115 章《入境條例》（「《條例》」）是以《國籍法》和《解釋》為基礎對中國公民作出定義。根據《條例》第 2 條，香港永久性居民即屬於附表 1 內指明的界別或者種類人士。

22　　而《條例》附表 1 第 2 條界定香港永久性居民為：

（a）在香港特別行政區成立以前或以後在香港出生的中國公民。

（b）在香港特別行政區成立以前或以後通常居於香港連續 7 年或以上的中國公民。

（c）中國公民在香港特別行政區成立以前或以後在香港以外所生的中國籍子女，而在該子女出生時，該中國公民是符合（a）或（b）項規定的人。

（d）在香港特別行政區成立以前或以後持有效旅行證件進入香港、通常居於香港連續 7 年或以上並以香港為永久居住地的非中國籍的人。

（e）在香港特別行政區成立以前或以後（d）項的香港特別行政區永久性居民在香港所生的未滿 21

歲的子女，而在該子女出生時或年滿 21 歲前任何時間，其父親或母親已享有香港居留權。

（f）（a）至（e）項的居民以外在香港特別行政區成立以前只在香港有居留權的人。

23　　這個對香港永久性居民的定義，基本是以《基本法》第 24 條作為藍本，唯獨對應《基本法》第 24 條（三）項的第 2（c）條和（五）項的第 2（e）條，對原文內容擴大了解釋。第 2（c）條將「在香港以外所生的中國籍子女」擴大解釋為「而在該子女出生時，該中國公民是符合（a）或（b）項規定的人」；而第 2（e）條則將「在香港出生的未滿 21 周歲的子女」變成「在香港所生的未滿 21 歲的子女，而在該子女出生時或年滿 21 歲前任何時間，其父親或母親已享有香港居留權」。第 2（c）條增加的解釋似乎仍然違背終審法院在陳錦雅 [11] 一案的裁定，無論怎樣，終審法院在該案的判詞從邏輯上實質支持第 2（e）條中增加的解釋，不需要子女出生時其父母便滿足《基本法》第 24 條（四）項擁有香港永久性居民身份這要求，只需要在其滿 21 周歲前能滿足這要件就可以。

24　　用同樣的邏輯思維，任何人士只要是在香港出生，哪怕他出生時因為不是中國公民而沒資格獲得香港永久性居民身份，然而只要他後來拿到中國公民身份便可依據《基本法》第 24 條（一）項而獲得香港永久居留權。

進一步以此思維比較（二）和（四）項，前者是在香港連續居住 7 年的中國公民，後者是非中國籍人士，只要（四）項人士拿到中國國籍變成中國公民後，他們也順理成章應被歸納為（二）項人士而無需以香港作為永久居住地而能維持其永久居留權。

因此，可以推論入境事務處的立場是香港永久性居民身份的獲得，是會因應相關人士的國籍或者身份的改變而變更。

香港永久居留權的喪失

至於永久居留權的喪失，根據香港法例第 115 章《入境條例》附表 1 包含如下情況：-

（一）第 4（1）條規定：「就第 2（e）段而言，該段所指的人在年滿 21 歲時，即不再是香港特別行政區永久性居民……。」

（二）根據過渡性條文第 6（2）的要求「任何屬中國公民且在緊接 1997 年 7 月 1 日前根據當時有效的本條例屬香港永久性居民的人，只要他仍是中國公民，即屬香港特別行政區永久性居民」；因此，當此類香港永久性居民在過渡特區政府管治時失去中國公民身份時，亦會同時失去香港永久性居民的身份。

（三）第 2（d）、2（e）及 2（f）段所指的人有連

續 36 個月以上不在香港，就有機會喪失香港永久性
居民身份。

《入境條例》不合理的情況

28　　　根據前文所述的現行政策，入境事務處雖然接受身
份是可以改變的事實，但是中國公民身份只要求在申請香
港永久性居民身份時擁有就可以，將來的註銷似乎不影響
已取得的香港永久性居民身份。

29　　　一方面將第 2（e）段的 21 周歲作為擁有香港永久性
居民身份的必要條件，當此條件不能滿足時就自動失去香
港永久性居民身份，可是對於第 2（a）及（b）段所要求
的中國公民條件，僅在申請獲取永久性居民身份才考慮，
往後這中國公民身份的註銷並不影響早前獲取的香港永久
性居民身份。

30　　　如果中國籍是中國公民的必然條件，中國籍的註銷
理應也是中國公民身份的喪失；為何在考慮香港永久性居
民身份時，中國公民的身份僅在申請或者出生時才考慮，
往後的註銷也不影響由此而得到的香港永久性居民身份？
反而一個較為次要的 21 周歲條件，在超越界限就會馬上
註銷已經獲取的香港永久性居民身份，道理上明顯輕重不
分，結果完全不合乎比例。

31　　　香港特區是中國的一部分，如果香港永久性居民的

身份是因為擁有中國公民才取得，從常埋來說，當中國公民這地位喪失後，由此而得到的香港永久性居民身份也應一併喪失。

32　　《基本法》裡也看不出有哪條賦予取得香港永久性居民身份的人士，在失去中國公民身份後還可以保留該永久性居民身份的權利。如前文所指出，只要將「中國公民」的要件改為「中國血統」或者「中國裔」便能達到這個目的，可是《基本法》並非這樣表述。

33　　所以，對於這類已經移居海外並獲得外國國籍的人士，入境事務處繼續讓他們行使香港永久性居民的權利是違背《基本法》的立法意圖，是行政不作為，必須盡快糾正。

補救措施

34　　回歸 20 多年，如果一直採納的標準或者政策突然改變，必然會影響很多人以及家庭。雖然坊間籠統的說《基本法》保證回歸後 50 年不變，然而，細心閱讀《基本法》總則第 5 條，「香港特別行政區不實行社會主義制度和政策，保持原有的資本主義制度和生活方式，五十年不變」，所謂的 50 年不變保證並不是說特區政府的施政政策在這段期間一成不變。事實上，《基本法》第 11 條已經明確指出在香港實施的所有的制度和政策均以《基本法》的規定為依據，任何制定的法律不能與其相抵觸。因此，香港特區入境事務處有責任糾正任何與《基本法》的立法意圖和目的相違背的出入境政策和法律。

35　　誠然，在執行和查證上會有一定困難，尤其是那些已經移居海外的前香港永久性居民。根據現行法律，他們現在所持有的香港永久性居民身份證註明了他們可以有進入香港並在港居留的權利。因此必須制定一套有效及可操作的程序，例如行使香港法例第 177 章《人事登記條例》第 7 條賦予的權力，識別這些已經喪失香港永久性居民身份的移民人士。

36　　另一方面，政策不能有雙重標準，以避免公眾批評有差別性的處理手法。因此，入境事務處也需要思考怎樣處理擁有居英權人士的香港永久性居民身份的問題。從務實的角度考慮，他們仍然在香港生活，居英權對他們來說可能僅僅是一本英國護照而已。而從理論層面考慮，這個英國國籍身份問題，是否實際上取代了他們中國公民的地位也不能完全確認，任何政策上的決定亦必須建立在《國籍法》的解釋上。

37　　然而，如前文所述，香港永久性居民身份的改變只會出現在同時失去地域上的聯繫和身份上的聯繫。所以，現實上那些因居英權政策而擁有英國國籍並仍然居於香港的人士，並不會因為其國籍問題而影響他們已經獲取的香港永久性居民身份。從實務的角度出發，這類人士不應該是被針對的類別人士；從緩急輕重上考慮，那些已經移居海外，只是繳納稅款予外地政府的人，是否應該讓他們繼續保留香港永久性居民身份的保障，才是問題的癥結。此外，也是向現在那些對移民趨之若鶩的人的當頭棒喝，讓他們在做任何決定前有再三思利害關係的機會。

註釋

1　根據英國政府通過的《英國（香港）國籍條例 1990》第 1 條，賦予居英權人士必須於回歸前登記為英國公民，從而享有自由進出和居住英國的權利。

2　香港法例第 115 條《入境條例 1972》附表 1 第 1 條對香港永久性居民的解釋為：「純粹為華人血統或帶有華人血統並曾在任何時間至少連續 7 年通常居於香港的人。」從字面上理解，血統是永遠不變的事實，而曾經在「任何時段連續 7 年居於香港」也是一個不可改變的事實，因此，邏輯上因滿足這個條件而獲得的永久性居民身份是永遠不可能會失去的。

3　入境事務處處長 對 莊豐源；FACV 26/2000。

4　吳嘉玲、吳丹丹 對 入境事務處處長；FACV 16/1998；談雅然、陳偉華 對 入境事務處處長；FACV 21/2000。

5　入境事務處處長 對 劉芳；FACV 10/2003

6　Gutierrez Josephine B. 對 人事登記處處長及人事登記審裁處；HCAL 136/2010

7　Maura Juliet A. Raquiza 對 入境事務處處長；CACV 272/2006。

8　The Law Reform Commission of Hong Kong's Report on Extrinsic Materials as an Aid to Statutory Interpretation, March 1997,（http://www.hkreform.gov.hk），第一章；see also Tandon v. Trustees of Spurgeon's Homes [1982] AC 755, 理論上法條裡也有機會存在沒意義的多餘字句，但是必須窮一切努力也找不出任何滿意的答案才會得出這結論。

9　見《入境條例》附表 1 第 4（1）條。

10　陳錦雅及其他 80 人 對 入境事務處處長；FACV 13/1998

11　見註 6。

II

英國政府對 BNO 護照的新政策

英國政府於 2021 年初開始實施一項新政策，為那些持有英國國民（海外）護照（簡稱 BNO 護照）的香港市民提供快速通道獲得英國公民身份。這種表面上出於為香港人權利的做法，其實質是外交政治上別有用心的考慮。這種偽善行為，可以從英國政府簽發 BNO 護照給香港市民的歷史背景加以說明。

策劃取消香港人既有的權利

在 1979 年《中英聯合聲明》開始談判之前，英國視香港為其殖民地。因此根據 1948 年《英國國籍法 1948》（British Nationality Act 1948）[12] 第 4 條，在此後出生的所有香港人原則上應自動有權獲得英國國籍。英國國會在 1977 年仍在綠皮書階段，討論應否改變一直沿用的國籍法 [13]。可能是預期中國將會恢復對香港行使主權，數年間迅速地完成了整個立法過程，並於 1981 年通過了《英國國籍法 1981》（British Nationality Act 1981）[14]，特別將香港歸納為一個新的類別，稱為英國屬地（British Dependent Territories），而不再視之為一個傳統的殖民地。根據《英國國籍法 1981》第 4 條，只有在英國居住和定居了不少於 5 年，期間不可離開英國本土超過 450 天的英國屬地公民（British Depandent Territories Citizen, BDTC），才可以登記成為英國公民。因此，BDTC 不再被納入在《移民法 1971》（Immigration Act 1971）[15] 第 2 條而享有英國公民通常擁有的居留權。這個 1981 年版本的立法，不但終止如《英國國籍法 1948》般將香港市民視為英國子民，而且還直接取消了香港市民根據其第 4 條和第 12 條獲得英國國籍的權利。

　　BNO 的概念於 1984 年 12 月簽署《中英聯合聲明》後才出現，並以 1986 年《香港（英國國籍）令》〔Hong Kong (British Nationality) Order 1986〕[16] 賦予法律地位，而該命令亦相應地修改了《英國國籍法 1981》。此外，根據《香港（英國國籍）（修訂）令 1993》〔Hong Kong (British Nationality) (Amendment) Order 1993〕[17]，在 1997 年 12 月 31 日之後將不再受理 BNO 的登記申請，這也符合《中英聯合聲明》中的約定[18]。然而，在 1997 年香港回歸中國後，根據 2002 年通過的《英國海外領土法 2002》（British Overseas Territories Act 2002）[19]，一夜間幾乎所有英國海外領土的公民全被授予完整的英國國籍，終結了過去數十年有關歧視英國海外領土居民的辯論或批評。然而，這種事情只在香港回歸後才發生，如此精心設計以防止香港人獲取英國國籍的權利，也可以在不同階段簽發給香港人的護照的內容中一一呈現出來。

不同時期英國護照的內容

41　　在 BDTC 護照中，BDTC 不再被稱為英國子民，但仍被稱為具有英國國籍的英國國民。在上世紀 80 年代初期及《香港（英國國籍）令 1986》宣佈之前，舊式 BDTC 護照的背面註釋頁上沒有具體提及持有人的居留權。可是，到 90 年代的護照，該頁的註釋 2 清楚地將英國公民與英國國民區分開來。因此，雖然護照持有人法律上是英國國民，但不論持有人是 BDTC 還是 BNO，都沒有英國的居留權。註釋 6 更進一步闡述，儘管英國允許雙重國籍（dual nationality）[20]，但對於雙重國籍的國民將不提供任何幫助。雖然 BNO 護照的內容與新款的 BDTC 護照內容相似，但事實上，該護照持有人已不再被視為英國子民或國民。至此，持有 BNO 護照的人只有在不超過 6 個月且僅為旅遊目的的情況下，才無需提前申請簽證而被允許進入英國逗留[21]。這一連串的改變，顯示了英國政府如何在香港回歸前，精心設計放棄曾經被他們口中聲稱為子民的香港人，及採取措施終止過去他們原有的權利。

多樣的英國國籍

42　　根據英國國籍法，當個人獲得國籍後，它將永久存在，直到被放棄或被剝奪為止，例如根據《英國國籍法

1981》第 40 條，子民的言論或行為被視為不忠於英國女王陛下。因此，雖然個人持有的 BNO 護照可能已過期，除非持有人主動取消其國籍或依據《英國國籍法》而被取消，持有 BNO 的身份應保持不變。而從放棄國籍和恢復國籍的規定推論，以及簽發的護照中明確的條文，英國是允許具有多重國籍的。可是，BNO 所指的國籍和中國法律規定的國籍性質有明顯的差別。中國公民就是中國市民，反之亦然，這種身份充分體現了國家及國民之間的權利和義務。然而，英國的相關情況卻有所不同。英國把國籍分為不同類別，將不同英國護照的種類區分了不同的權利，由擁有居留權的完整英國公民權利，到僅提供海外領事援助都有。BNO 持有人擁有的權利，顯然遠不及英國公民所享有的權利。這種安排毫無疑問對 BNO 護照持有人是歧視性待遇。可是，就用語而言，這仍然難以質疑其持有人是英國國民的身份，並且是英國國籍的持有者。此外，從英國各種國籍立法的仔細研究可以得知，即使有不同的國籍類別，它們都是建基於對英國王室的依附、忠誠和效忠。因此，無論是概念上還是實質上的結論，持有 BNO 的中國公民必然會構成違反《中華人民共和國國籍法》有關禁止雙重國籍的規定。後果是持有人將被視為已放棄中國國籍，或者對於因為香港的聯繫而獲得的 BNO 國籍將不會被中國政府承認。在《中英聯合聲明》的中方備忘錄中明確承認了這種困境。在該備忘錄裡，中國政府一方面再次強調了《中國國籍法》的重要性；另一方面，亦清晰表明持有 BNO 護照不會損害持有人的中國國籍。因此，從邏輯上推論，這意味著中國政府僅將 BNO 護照視為旅行證件，而不涉及國籍範疇。

對於本地媒體最近報導 BNO 護照申請和簽發數量有激增的情況應被小心地理解。所有 BNO 護照的申請均應根據《香港（英國國籍）（修訂）令 1993》或《中英聯合聲明》裡所同意的，須於 1997 年 12 月 31 日或之前提出。可是，《中英聯合聲明》的英方備忘錄的第（c）條指出，1997 年 7 月 1 日之前出生且已被納入其父母護照的人，可以在 1997 年 12 月 31 日之後向英國駐香港的領事官員申請 BNO 護照。從有關條款的字面解釋，申請必須在 1997 年 12 月 31 日或之前提出，或者申請者是在 1997 年 7 月 1 日之前出生並已經包括在其父母的護照中，否則 BNO 護照並不會在 1997 年 12 月 31 日截止日期之後簽發。簡而言之，除了出生於 1997 年 7 月 1 日之前且未申請登記但其姓名已加註在其父母的 BNO 護照中的人，英國政府不得在 1997 年 12 月 31 日之後接受任何新的 BNO 護照申請。任何聲稱英國政府已通過新政策允許任何香港人申請 BNO 護照的說法，都是不正確的。即使是當年有權申請但未在截止日期前申請的香港人，也不能現在提出申請。從歷史上看，在開始與中國談判恢復對香港行使主權之前，英國政府已經計劃取消其海外領土公民能夠得到全面英國國籍的權利。支持英國政府進行這計劃的人宣稱，此等安排是為了避免 1997 年回歸時，有機會出現大量湧入英國本土的香港移民。無論如何，這清楚說明《英國國籍法 1981》實際上是針對香港。

當年這項計劃在英國其實亦面對不少質疑及挑戰，嚴厲的批評認為英國政府沒有對海外領土的子民承擔最低限度的道德責任。爭議持續到「六四事件」達到了最高點。然而，英國政府堅決進行此後過渡期的國籍安排，並在 1993 年實施該計劃的最後一步，通過《香港（英國國籍）（修訂）令 1993》。緊接著 1997 年香港回歸，特別是當大規模移民的風險解決之後，英國政府再通過了另一項立法，即 2002 年的《英國海外領土法 2002》（British Overseas Territories Act 2002），將居留權擴展到其大部分海外領土。顯而易見，英國政府從來不曾重視過香港居民在回歸後的福祉。相反，其針對性政策顯露出，英國只將自身利益放在首位。至於英國國籍甄選計劃提供的 50,000 個配額 [22]（《居英權計劃》）應只被視為一種政治策略，目的是在 1997 年英國永久退出香港之前，盡量從香港吸納富裕的中產階級和精英階層，帶回到英國。而英國政府最近的新政策實際上是另一次算計，類似於 30 年前的《居英權計劃》，目的是再次將中產階級或精英階層從香港吸走。從開始談判《中英聯合聲明》，英國政府已暗中修改立法防止香港市民大量移民到英國本土。而這次所謂對需要保護的人提供幫助的新政策，也只是一個漂亮的外交藉口而已。

誤導的新政策

45
事實上，根據宣佈的新政策，受援助的人群並不是最弱勢或無助的人，而是那些在 1997 年 7 月 1 日之前出生並獲得認可的 BNO 身份的人。這類人羣應該是社會的菁英，起碼也是已經完成學業並將為勞動市場作出最大貢獻的人。除了獲得 5 年的工作或求學簽證外，在新政策下英國政府不會以任何方式補助他們。在這段漫長的時間中他們必須自力更生並持續為英國經濟作出貢獻。5 年後需再申請多留在英國一年，才能獲得長久的居留許可。對於英國政府來說，這個安排幾乎是無本生利，不需花一分錢就能得到優質的勞動力。

46
儘管英國政府進行了這種名不符實的外交宣傳，但僅通過對香港人或香港特定階層的人提供一些移民優惠而指責它違反《中英聯合聲明》可能也有些牽強，尤其《中英聯合聲明》中並沒有這樣的義務或承諾，即自 1997 年以後永遠排除或禁止香港人移民英國。極其量，我們只可從《中英聯合聲明》的英方備忘錄中的第 (a) 和 (b) 條得出英國承諾不會僅僅因為與香港有聯繫而授予香港市民英國公民的身份 23。歸根究底，控制移民政策是任何主權國的特有權力。英國政府可在不參考其他國家情況下，完全自主制定此類內部政策。當然，將這項政策與 BNO 護照持有人身份聯繫起來是完全沒有必要的，而且帶有嚴重的誤導性，由此不難看出這政治行為背後的動機。

註 釋

12 https://www.legislation.gov.uk/ukpga/Geo6/11-12/56/contents/enacted

13 1977 年 4 月 27 日英國國會討論記錄；https://api.parliament.uk/historic-hansard/commons/1977/apr/27/british-nationality-law

14 https://www.legislation.gov.uk/ukpga/1981/61/contents

15 https://www.legislation.gov.uk/ukpga/1971/77/section/3

16 https://www.legislation.gov.uk/uksi/1986/948/contents/made

17 https://www.legislation.gov.uk/uksi/1993/1795/made

18 《中英聯合聲明》英方備忘錄第 (b) 條

19 https://www.legislation.gov.uk/ukpga/2002/8/contents

20 不少國家如日本和新加坡也不允許雙重國籍，其中原因包括領事保護、國家效忠和公民責任方面的矛盾。

21 https://www.gov.uk/check-uk-visa/y/british-national-overseas/tourism

22 https://www.legislation.gov.uk/uksi/1990/2292/made

23 https://www.cmab.gov.hk/en/issues/jd6.htm

附錄

香港法例第 115 章《入境條例 1972》附表 1 第 4（1）條

附表 1

4. 第 2（e）段下的永久性居民身分的確立

（1）就第 2（e）段而言，該段所指的人在年滿 21 歲時，即不再是香港特別行政區永久性居民，但可隨時向處長申請根據第 2（d）段獲得香港特別行政區永久性居民身分。

《中英聯合聲明》中、英雙方備忘錄

備忘錄（英方）

聯繫到今天簽訂的大不列顛及北愛爾蘭聯合王國政府和中華人民共和國政府關於香港問題的聯合聲明，聯合王國政府聲明，在完成對聯合王國有關立法的必要修改的情況下，

一、凡根據聯合王國實行的法律，在 1997 年 6 月 30 日由於同香港的關係為英國屬土公民者，從 1997 年 7 月 1 日起，不再是英國屬土公民，但將有資格保留某種適當地位，使其可繼續使用聯合王國政府簽發的護照，而不賦予在聯合王國的居留權。取得這種地位的人，必須為持有在 1997 年 7 月 1 日以前簽發的該種英國護照或包括在該種護照上的人，但 1997 年 1 月 1 日或該日以後、1997 年 7 月 1 日以前出生的有資格的人，可在 1997 年 12 月 31 日截止的期間內取得該種護照或包括在該種護照上。

二、在 1997 年 7 月 1 日或該日以後，任何人不得由於同香港的關係而取得英國屬土公民的地位。凡在 1997 年 7 月 1 日或該日以後出生者，不得取得第一節中所述的適當地位。

三、在香港特別行政區和其他地方的聯合王國的領事官員可為第一節中提及的人所持的護照延長期限和予以更換，亦可給他們在 1997 年 7 月 1 日前出生並且原來包括在他們護照上的子女簽發護照。

四、根據第一節和第二節已領取聯合王國政府簽發的護照的人或包括在該護照上的人，經請求有權在第三國獲得英國的領事服務和保護。

英國駐華大使館（印）

1984 年 12 月 19 日

備忘錄（中方）

中華人民共和國政府收到了大不列顛及北愛爾蘭聯合王國政府 1984 年 12 月 19 日的備忘錄。

根據中華人民共和國國籍法，所有香港中國同胞，不論其是否持有「英國屬土公民護照」，都是中國公民。

考慮到香港的歷史背景和現實情況，中華人民共和國政府主管部門自 1997 年 7 月 1 日起，允許原被稱為「英國屬土公民」的香港中國公民使用由聯合王國政府簽發的旅行證件去其他國家和地區旅行。

上述中國公民在香港特別行政區和中華人民共和國其他地區不得因其持有上述英國旅行證件而享受英國的領事保護的權利。

中華人民共和國外交部（印）

1984 年 12 月 19 日

《英國國籍法 1948》第 4 條和第 12 條

4. Citizenship by birth

Subject to the provisions of this section, every person born within the United Kingdom and Colonies after the commencement of this Act shall be a citizen of the United Kingdom and Colonies by birth :

Provided that a person shall not be such a citizen by virtue of this section if at the time of his birth—

(a) his father possesses such immunity from suit and legal process as is accorded to an envoy of a foreign sovereign power accredited to His Majesty, and is not a citizen of the United Kingdom and Colonies; or

(b) his father is an enemy alien and the birth occurs in a place then under occupation by the enemy.

12. British subjects before commencement of Act becoming citizens of United Kingdom and Colonies

(1) A person who was a British subject immediately before the date of the commencement of this Act shall on that date become a citizen of the United Kingdom and Colonies if he possesses any of the following qualifications, that is to say—

(a) that he was born within the territories comprised at the commencement of this Act in the United Kingdom and Colonies, and would have been such a citizen if section four of this Act had been in force at the time of his birth;

(b) that he is a person naturalised in the United Kingdom and Colonies;

(c) that he became a British subject by reason of the annexation of any territory included at the commencement of this Act in the United Kingdom and Colonies.

(2) A person who was a British subject immediately before the date of the commencement of this Act shall on that date become a citizen of the United Kingdom and Colonies if at the time of his birth his father was a British subject and possessed any of the qualifications specified in the last foregoing subsection.

(3) A person who was a British subject immediately before the date of the commencement of this Act shall on that date become a citizen of the United Kingdom and Colonies if he was born within the territory comprised at the commencement of this Act in a protectorate, protected state or United Kingdom trust territory.

(4) A person who was a British subject immediately before the date of the commencement of this Act and does not become a citizen of the United Kingdom and Colonies by virtue of any of the foregoing provisions of this section shall on that date become such a citizen unless—

(a) he is then a citizen of any country mentioned in subsection (3) of section one of this Act under a citizenship law having effect in that country, or a citizen of Eire ; or

(b) he is then potentially a citizen of any country mentioned in subsection (3) of section one of this Act.

(5) A woman who was a British subject immediately before the date of the commencement of this Act and has before that date been married to a person who becomes, or would but for his death have become, a citizen of the United Kingdom and Colonies by virtue of any of the foregoing provisions of this section shall on that date herself become such a citizen.

(6) If any person of full age and capacity who would have become a citizen of the United Kingdom and Colonies on the date of the commencement of this Act by virtue of subsection (4) of this section but for his citizenship or potential citizenship of any country mentioned in subsection (3) of section one of this Act makes application to the Secretary of State in the prescribed manner before the first day of January nineteen hundred and fifty for the registration of himself and any

of his minor children as citizens of the United Kingdom and Colonies, and on such application satisfies the Secretary of State—

(a) that he is descended in the male line from a person possessing any of the qualifications specified in subsection (1) of this section ; and

(b) that he intends to make his ordinary place of residence within the United Kingdom and Colonies,

then, if it seems to the Secretary of State fitting that that person should by reason of his close connection with the United Kingdom and Colonies become a citizen thereof, the Secretary of State may cause him, and any minor children to whom the application relates, to be registered as such; and that person, and any such minor children as aforesaid, shall thereupon become citizens of the United Kingdom and Colonies.

(7) The Secretary of State may make arrangements for the exercise in any country mentioned in subsection (3) of section one of this Act of any of his functions under the last foregoing subsection by the High Commissioner for His Majesty's government in the United Kingdom.

(8) A male person who becomes a citizen of the United Kingdom and Colonies by virtue only of subsection (2), (4) or (6) of this section shall be deemed for the purposes of the proviso to subsection (1) of section five of this Act to be a citizen of the United Kingdom and Colonies by descent only.

《移民法 1971》第 2 條

2. Statement of right of abode, and related amendments as to citizenship by registration

(1) A person is under this Act to have the right of abode in the United Kingdom if—

(a) he is a citizen of the United Kingdom and Colonies who has that citizenship by his birth, adoption, naturalisation or (except as mentioned below) registration in the United Kingdom or in any of the Islands; or

(b) he is a citizen of the United Kingdom and Colonies born to or legally adopted by a parent who had that citizenship at the time of the birth or adoption, and the parent either—

(i) then had that citizenship by his birth, adoption, naturalisation or (except as mentioned below) registration in the United Kingdom or in any of the Islands; or

(ii) had been born to or legally adopted by a parent who at the time of that birth or adoption so had it; or

(c) he is a citizen of the United Kingdom and Colonies who has at any time been settled in the United Kingdom and Islands and had at that time (and while such a citizen) been ordinarily resident there for the last five years or more ; or

(d) he is a Commonwealth citizen born to or legally adopted by a parent who at the time of the birth or adoption had citizenship of the United Kingdom and Colonies by his birth in the United Kingdom or in any of the Islands.

(2) A woman is under this Act also to have the right of abode in the United Kingdom if she is a Commonwealth citizen and either—

(a) is the wife of any such citizen of the United Kingdom and Colonies as is mentioned in subsection (1)(a), (b) or (c) above or any such Commonwealth citizen as is mentioned in subsection (1)(d); or

(b) has at any time been the wife—

(i) of a person then being such a citizen of the United Kingdom and Colonies or Commonwealth citizen; or

(ii) of a British subject who but for his death would on the date of commencement of the [1948 c. 56.] British Nationality Act 1948 have been such a citizen of the United Kingdom and Colonies as is mentioned in subsection (1)(a) or (b);

but in subsection (1)(a) and (b) above references to registration as a citizen of the United Kingdom and Colonies shall not, in the case of a woman, include registration after the passing of this Act under or by virtue of section 6(2) (wives) of the British Nationality Act 1948 unless she is so registered by virtue of her marriage to a citizen of the United Kingdom and Colonies before the passing of this Act.

(3) In relation to the parent of a child born after the parent's death, references in subsection (1) above to the time of the child's birth shall be replaced by references to the time of the parent's death; and for purposes of that subsection—

(a) " parent" includes the mother of an illegitimate child; and

(b) references to birth in the United Kingdom shall include birth on a ship or aircraft registered in the United Kingdom, or on an unregistered ship or aircraft of the Government of the United Kingdom, and similarly with references to birth in any of the Islands; and

(c) references to citizenship of the United Kingdom and Colonies shall, in relation to a time before the year 1949, be construed as references to British nationality and, in relation to British nationality and to a time before the 31st March 1922, "the United Kingdom" shall mean Great Britain and Ireland ; and

(d) subject to section 8(5) below, references to a person being settled in the United Kingdom and Islands are references to his being ordinarily resident there without being subject under the immigration laws to any restriction on the period for which he may remain.

(4) In subsection (1) above, any reference to registration in the United Kingdom shall extend also to registration under arrangements made by virtue of section 8(2) of the [1948 c. 56.] British Nationality Act 1948 (registration in independent Commonwealth country by United Kingdom High Commissioner), but, in the case of a registration by virtue of section 7 (children) of that Act, only if the registration was effected before the passing of this Act.

(5) The law with respect to registration as a citizen of the United Kingdom and Colonies shall be modified as provided by Schedule 1 to this Act.

(6) In the following provisions of this Act the word " patrial " is used of persons having the right of abode in the United Kingdom.

《英國國籍法 1981》第 4 條和第 40 條

4. Acquisition by registration: British Dependent Territories citizens etc.

(1) This section applies to any person who is a British Dependent Territories citizen, a British Overseas citizen, a British subject under this Act or a British protected person.

(2) A person to whom this section applies shall be entitled, on an application for his registration as a British citizen, to be registered as such a citizen if the following requirements are satisfied in the case of that person, namely—

(a) subject to subsection (3), that he was in the United Kingdom at the beginning of the period of five years ending with the date of the application and that the number of days on which he was absent from the United Kingdom in that period does not exceed 450 ; and

(b) that the number of days on which he was absent from the United Kingdom in the period of twelve months so ending does not exceed 90 ; and

(c) that he was not at any time in the period of twelve months so ending subject under the immigration laws to any restriction on the period for which he might remain in the United Kingdom ; and

(d) that he was not at any time in the period of five years so ending in the United Kingdom in breach of the immigration laws.

(3) So much of subsection (2)(a) as requires the person in question to have been in the United Kingdom at the beginning of the period there mentioned shall not apply in relation to a person who was settled in the United Kingdom immediately before commencement.

(4) If in the special circumstances of any particular case the Secretary of State thinks fit, he may for the purposes of subsection (2) do all or any of the following things, namely—

(a) treat the person to whom the application relates as fulfilling the requirement specified in subsection (2) (a) or subsection (2)(b), or both, although the number of days on which he was absent from the United Kingdom in the period there mentioned exceeds the number there mentioned;

(b) disregard any such restriction as is mentioned in subsection (2) (c), not being a restriction to which that person was subject on the date of the application ;

(c) treat that person as fulfilling the requirement specified in subsection (2)(d) although he was in the United Kingdom in breach of the immigration laws in the period there mentioned.

(5) If, on an application for registration as a British citizen made by a person to whom this section applies, the Secretary of State is satisfied that the applicant has at any time served in service to which this subsection applies, he may, if he thinks fit in the special circumstances of the applicant's case, cause him to be registered as such a citizen.

(6) Subsection (5) applies to—

(a) Crown service under the government of a dependent territory; and

(b) paid or unpaid service (not falling within paragraph (a)) as a member of any body established by law in a dependent territory members of which are appointed by or on behalf of the Crown.

40. Deprivation of citizenship

(1) Subject to the provisions of this section, the Secretary of State may by order deprive any British citizen to whom this subsection applies of his British citzenship if the Secretary of State is satisfied that the registration or certificate of naturalisation by virtue of which he is such a citizen was obtained by means of fraud, false representation or the concealment of any material fact.

(2) Subsection (1) applies to any British citizen who—

(a) became a British citizen after commencement by virtue of—

(i) his registration as a British citizen under any provision of this Act; or

(ii) a certificate of naturalisation granted to him under section 6 ; or

(b) being immediately before commencement a citizen of the United Kingdom and Colonies by virtue of registration as such a citizen under any provision of the British Nationality Acts 1948 to 1964, became at commencement a British citizen ; or

(c) at any time before commencement became a British subject (within the meaning of that expression at that time), or a citizen of Eire or of the Republic of Ireland, by virtue of a certificate of naturalisation granted to him or in which his name was included.

(3) Subject to the provisions of this section, the Secretary of State may by order deprive any British citizen to whom this subsection applies of his British citizenship if the Secretary of State is satisfied that that citizen—

(a) has shown himself by act or speech to be disloyal or disaffected towards Her Majesty ; or

(b) has, during any war in which Her Majesty was engaged, unlawfully traded or communicated with an enemy or been engaged in or associated with any business that was to his knowledge carried on in such a manner as to assist an enemy in that war ; or

(c) has, within the period of five years from the relevant date, been sentenced in any country to imprisonment for a term of not less than twelve months.

(4) Subsection (3) applies to any British citizen who falls within paragraph (a) or (c) of subsection (2); and in subsection (3) " the relevant date ", in relation to a British citizen to whom subsection (3) applies, means the date of the registration by virtue of which he is such a citizen or, as the case may be, the date of the grant of the certificate of naturalisation by virtue of which he is such a citizen.

(5) The Secretary of State—

(a) shall not deprive a person of British citizenship under this section unless he is satisfied that it is not conducive to the public good that that person should continue to be a British citizen ; and

(b) shall not deprive a person of British citizenship under subsection (3) on the ground mentioned in paragraph (c) of that subsection if it appears to him that that person would thereupon become stateless.

(6) Before making an order under this section the Secretary of State shall give the person against whom the order is proposed to be made notice in writing informing him of the ground or grounds on which it is proposed to be made and of his right to an inquiry under this section.

(7) If the person against whom the order is proposed to be made applies in the prescribed manner for an inquiry, the Secretary of State shall, and in any other case the Secretary of State may, refer the case to a committee of inquiry consisting of a chairman, being a person possessing judicial experience, appointed by the Secretary of State and of such other members appointed by the Secretary of State as he thinks proper.

(8) The Secretary of State may make rules for the practice and procedure to be followed in connection with references under subsection (7) to a committee of inquiry; and such rules may, in particular, provide for conferring on any such committee any powers, rights or privileges of any court, and for enabling any powers so conferred to be exercised by one or more members of the committee.

(9) The power of the Secretary of State to make rules under subsection (8) shall be exercisable by statutory instrument subject to annulment in pursuance of a resolution of either House of Parliament.

(10) The preceding provisions of this section shall apply in relation to British Dependent Territories citizens and British Dependent Territories citizenship as they apply in relation to British citizens and British citizenship, but as if in subsection (2)(a)(ii) the reference to section 6 were a reference to section 18.

《香港（英國國籍）令 1986》

Statutory Instruments

1986 No. 948

BRITISH NATIONALITY

The Hong Kong (British Nationality) Order 1986

Laid before Parliament in draft

Made

5th June 1986

Coming into Operation

1st July 1987

At the Court at Buckingham Palace, the 5th day of June 1986

Present,

The Queen's Most Excellent Majesty in Council

Whereas a draft of this Order has been laid before Parliament and has been approved by a resolution of each House of Parliament:

Now, therefore, Her Majesty, in pursuance of paragraph 2 of the Schedule to the Hong Kong Act 1985, is pleased, by and with the advice of Her Privy Council, to order, and it is hereby ordered, as follows:—

Citation, commencement, extent and interpretation

1.—(1) This Order may be cited as the Hong Kong (British Nationality) Order 1986 and shall come into operation on 1st July 1987.

(2) This Order extends to Northern Ireland.

(3) This Order extends to the Channel Islands and the Isle of Man and to all dependent territories.

(4) Section 50 of the British Nationality Act 1981 (interpretation) shall apply to the interpretation of this Order as it applies to the interpretation of that Act.

Connections with Hong Kong

2. —(1) For the purposes of this Order a person shall be taken to have a connection with Hong Kong if—

(a) subject to paragraph (3) below, he, his father or his mother was born, naturalised or registered in Hong Kong or found abandoned there as a new-born infant; or

(b) he, his father or his mother was adopted (whether or not in Hong Kong) and the adopter or, in the case of a joint adoption, one of the adopters was at the time of the adoption a British Dependent Territories citizen by virtue of his having a connection with Hong Kong as specified in this Article; or

(c) he, his father or his mother was registered outside Hong Kong on an application based (wholly or partly) on any of the following:—

(i) residence in Hong Kong;

(ii) descent from a person born in Hong Kong;

(iii) descent from a person naturalised, registered or settled in Hong Kong (whether before or after the birth of the person registered);

(iv) descent from a person adopted (whether or not in Hong Kong) in the circumstances specified in sub-paragraph (b) above;

(v) marriage to a person who is a British Dependent Territories citizen by virtue of his having a connection with Hong Kong as specified in this Article or would have been so but for his death or renunciation of citizenship;

(vi) Crown service under the government of Hong Kong;

(vii) where citizenship has been renounced and subsequently resumed, birth, naturalisation or registration in Hong Kong; or

(d) at the time of his birth his father or mother was settled in Hong Kong; or

(e) his father or mother was born to a parent who at the time of the birth was a citizen of the United Kingdom and Colonies by virtue of his having a connection with Hong Kong as specified in this Article; or

(f) being a woman, she was married before 1st January 1983 to a man who is a British Dependent Territories citizen by virtue of his having a connection with Hong Kong as specified in this Article or would have been so but for his death.

(2) In paragraph (1) above "registered" means registered as a British Dependent Territories citizen or, before 1st January 1983, as a citizen of the United Kingdom and Colonies; and "registration" shall be construed accordingly.

(3) A person born in Hong Kong on or after 1st January 1983 shall not be taken to have a connection with Hong Kong under paragraph (1) (a) above by virtue of his birth there unless, at the time of his birth, one of his parents was—

(a) settled in Hong Kong; or

(b) a British Dependent Territories citizen by virtue of his having a connection with Hong Kong as specified in this Article.

Loss of British Dependent Territories citizenship

3. Any person who, immediately before 1st July 1997—

(a) is a British Dependent Territories citizen by virtue (wholly or partly) of his having a connection with Hong Kong; and

(b) but for his having a connection with Hong Kong would not be a British Dependent Territories citizen, shall on that date cease to be such a citizen.

Right to acquire new status of British National (Overseas)

4.—(1) On and after 1st July 1987 there shall be a new form of British nationality the holders of which shall be known as British Nationals (Overseas).

(2) Any person who is a British Dependent Territories citizen by virtue (wholly or partly) of his having a connection with Hong Kong and who, but for his having a connection with Hong Kong, would not be such a citizen shall be entitled, before 1st July 1997 (or before the end of 1997 if born in that year before that date), to be registered as a British National (Overseas) and to hold or be included in a passport appropriate to that status.

(3) Any person who, having become a British National (Overseas) by virtue of paragraph (2) above, ceases at any time before 1st July 1997 to be a British Dependent Territories citizen shall at the same time cease to be a British National (Overseas).

Removal of Hong Kong from list of dependent territories

5. On and after 1st July 1997 the British Nationality Act 1981 shall have effect as if in Schedule 6 to that Act (British Dependent Territories) the words "Hong Kong" were omitted.

Provisions for reducing statelessness

6.—(1) Where a person ceases on 1st July 1997 by virtue of Article 3 to be a British Dependent Territories citizen and would, but for this paragraph, thereby be rendered stateless, he shall become on that date a British Overseas citizen.

(2) Where a person born on or after 1st July 1997 would, but for this paragraph, be born stateless, then, if at the time of the birth his father or mother is a British National (Overseas) or a British Overseas citizen by virtue of paragraph (1) above, he shall be a British Overseas citizen.

(3) A person born stateless on or after 1st July 1997 outside the dependent territories shall be entitled, on an application for his registration as a British Overseas citizen made within the period of twelve months from the date of the birth, to be registered as such a citizen if the requirements specified in paragraph (4) below are fulfilled in the case of either that person's father of his mother ("the parent in question").

(4) The requirements referred to in paragraph (3) above are—

(a) that the parent in question was a British Overseas citizen by virtue of paragraph (2) above at the time of the birth; and

(b) that the father or mother of the parent in question was, immediately before 1st July 1997, a British Dependent Territories citizen otherwise than by descent by virtue of having a connection with Hong Kong or would have been so but for his or her death.

(5) If in the special circumstances of any particular case the Secretary of State thinks fit, he may treat paragraph (3) above as if the reference to twelve months were a reference to six years.

British Nationality Acts

7.—(1) The British Nationality Act 1981 ("the 1981 Act") and the British Nationality (Falkland Islands) Act 1983 ("the 1983 Act") shall have effect subject to the following provisions of this Article.

(2) Section 4(1) of the 1981 Act (acquisition by registration: British Dependent Territories citizens, etc.) shall have effect as if after the words "British Dependent Territories citizen," there were inserted the words "a British National (Overseas),".

(3) Section 37 of the 1981 Act (Commonwealth citizenship) shall have effect as if in subsection (1) (a)—

(a) the reference to the 1981 Act included a reference to this Order;

(b) after the words "British Dependent Territories citizen," there were inserted the words "a British National (Overseas),".

(4) Section 41 of the 1981 Act (regulations and Orders in Council) shall have effect as if—

(a) any reference in it to the 1981 Act included a reference to this Order;

(b) in subsection (1)(f) after the word "citizenship" there were inserted the words "or of the status of a British National (Overseas)";

(c) in subsection (1)(i) after the words "British Dependent Territories citizens," there were inserted the words "British Nationals

(Overseas),";

(d) in subsection (2)—

(i) at the end of paragraph (a) there were inserted the words "other than an application for the purpose of acquiring the status of a British National (Overseas)";

(ii) at the end of paragraph (b) there were inserted the words "other than registration as a British National (Overseas)".

(5) Section 42 of the 1981 Act (registration and naturalisation: general provisions) shall have effect as if—

(a) in subsection (2)(b) after the words "British Dependent Territories citizen," there were inserted the words "a British National (Overseas),";

(b) in subsection (4)—

(i) the reference to the 1981 Act included a reference to this Order;

(ii) after the words "British Dependent Territories citizen" there were inserted the words ", or as a British National (Overseas),";

(iii) after the words "as the case may be," there were inserted the words "a British National (Overseas) or".

(6) Section 43 of the 1981 Act (exercise of functions of Secretary of State by Governors and others) shall have effect as if—

(a) any reference in it to the 1981 Act included a reference to this Order;

(b) in subsection (1)(b) at the end there were inserted the words "and in cases concerning British Nationals (Overseas) or the status of a British National (Overseas)";

(c) in subsection (2) at the end there were inserted the following paragraph:—

"(c)renunciation and deprivation of the status of a British National (Overseas).".

(7) The following provisions of the 1981 Act shall have effect as if any reference in them to the 1981 Act included a reference to this Order, namely—

(a) section 45 (evidence);

(b) section 46(1) (offences);

(c) sections 47 and 48 (legitimated and posthumous children).

(8) Section 50 of the 1981 Act (interpretation) shall have effect as if in paragraph (1) after the definition of "association" there were inserted the following definitions:—

"British National (Overseas)" means a person who is a British National (Overseas) under the Hong Kong (British Nationality) Order 1986, and "status of a British National (Overseas)" shall be construed accordingly;

"British Overseas citizen" includes a person who is a British Overseas citizen under the Hong Kong (British Nationality) Order 1986.

(9) Section 51 of the 1981 Act (meaning of certain expressions relating to nationality in other Acts and instruments) shall have effect as if in subsection (3)—

(a) at the end of paragraph (a)(ii) there were inserted the words "or who under the Hong Kong (British Nationality) Order 1986 is a British National (Overseas)";

(b) in paragraph (b) after the words "British Dependent Territories citizen" thre were inserted the words "nor a British National (Overseas)".

(10) The provisions of section 12 of the 1981 Act (renunciation) shall apply in relation to British Nationals (Overseas) and the status of a British National (Overseas) as they apply in relation to British citizens and British citizenship.

(11) The provisions of section 40 of the 1981 Act (deprivation of citizenship) shall apply in relation to persons registered as British Nationals (Overseas) under this Order and the status of a British National (Overseas) as they apply in relation to persons registered as British citizens under the 1981 Act and British citizenship.

(12) Section 2 of the 1983 Act (acquisition of British citizenship by registration) shall have effect as if—

(a) in subsection (1)(a) at the end there were inserted the words "or who, having become such a citizen by virtue of that section, is a British National (Overseas)";

(b) in subsection (2)(a) at the end there were inserted the words "or who, having become such a citizen by virtue of registration or naturalisation under the 1981 Act, is a British National (Overseas)".

Consequential amendments

8. The enactments specified in the Schedule to this Order shall have effect subject to the amendments there specified, being amendments consequential on the provisions of this Order.

《英國（香港）國籍條例 1990》第 1 條
British Nationality (Hong Kong) Act 1990
1990 CHAPTER 34

An Act to provide for the acquisition of British citizenship by selected Hong Kong residents, their spouses and minor children.

[26th July 1990]

WE IT ENACTED by the Queen's most Excellent Majesty, by and with the advice and consent of the Lords Spiritual and Temporal, and Commons, in this present Parliament assembled, and by the authority of the same, as follows:—

1. Acquisition of British citizenship

(1) Subject to the provisions of this section, the Secretary of State shall register as British citizens up to 50,000 persons recommended to him for that purpose by the Governor of Hong Kong under a scheme or schemes made and approved in accordance with Schedule 1 to this Act.

(2) No person shall be registered under subsection (1) above after 30th June 1997.

(3) The Secretary of State may direct the Governor to make not more than a specified proportion of his recommendations in a period or periods specified in the direction; and any such direction may make different provision in relation to recommendations in respect of persons of different classes or descriptions.

(4) Schedule 2 to this Act shall have effect for enabling the spouse and minor children of a person registered under subsection (1) above to acquire British citizenship by registration; and no spouse or minor

child to whom Schedule 2 to this Act applies shall be registered under subsection (1) above.

(5) Neither the Secretary of State nor the Governor shall be required to give any reason for any decision made by him in the exercise of a discretion vested in him by or under this Act and no such decision shall be subject to appeal or liable to be questioned in any court.

《英國（香港）（國籍甄選計劃）令》（《居英權計劃》）附件 1 至 4 及解釋

ANNEX 1 GENERAL OCCUPATIONAL CLASSSPECIFIED OCCUPATIONAL GROUPS

Article 7

1. Managers and administrators.

2. Business professionals.

3. Business and administration associate professionals.

4. Accountants and auditors.

5. Accounting associate professionals.

6. Engineers and related professionals.

7. Architects, planners and surveyors.

8. Engineering associate professionals.

9. Information science professionals.

10. News editors and journalists.

11. Medical doctors.

12. Physical and life science professionals.

13. Nurses and midwives.

14. Other medical professionals (except nurses and midwives).

15. Health associate professionals (except nurses and midwives).

16. Legal professionals.

17. Legal associate professionals.

18. Teaching professionals (post-secondary).

19. Educational administrators.

20. Other teaching personnel.

ANNEX 2 GENERAL OCCUPATIONAL CLASSAGE POINTS

Article 11(1)

Age	Points
20 or below	0
21	20
22	40
23	60
24	80
25	100
26	120
27	140
28	160
29	180
30 to 41	200
42	180
43	160
44	140
45	120
46	100
47	80
48	60
49	40
50	20
51	0
52	-20
53	-40
54	-60
55	-80
56	-100
57	-120
58	-140

Age	Points
59	-160
60	-180
61 and above	-200

ANNEX 3 GENERAL OCCUPATIONAL CLASSALLOCATION OF POINTS FOR EACH YEAR'S RELEVANT EXPERIENCE FOR THOSE APPLYING IN THE MANAGERS AND ADMINISTRATORS OCCUPATIONAL GROUP

Article 12(2)

Average annual earnings (in Hong Kong dollars)	Points for each year's experience
Under 200,000	1
200,000 – 224,999	2
225,000 – 249,999	3
250,000 – 299,999	4
300,000 – 349,999	5
350,000 – 399,999	6
400,000 – 599,999	7
600,000 – 999,999	8
1,000,000 – 1,999,999	9
2,000,000 or above	10

ANNEX 4 GENERAL OCCUPATIONAL CLASSPOINTS FOR PROFESSIONAL OR VOCATIONAL QUALIFICATIONS

Article 13(3)

Specified occupational group	Qualification	Points
1. Managers and administrators	Matriculation	25
	Post-secondary qualification (other than a degree)	35
	Bachelor degree or membership or fellowship of professional institution	50
2. Business professionals	Matriculation	25
	Post-secondary qualification (other than a degree) or associate membership of professional institution	35
	Bachelor degree or membership or fellowship of professional institution	50
3. Business and administration associate professionals	Matriculation	25
	Post-secondary qualification (other than a degree) or associate membership of professional institution	50
4. Accountants and auditors	Level I Professional Examination	15
	Bachelor degree in accountancy	20
	Level II Professional Examination	25
	Level III Professional Examination	40
	Membership or fellowship of professional institution	50

Specified occupational group	Qualification	Points
5. Accounting associate professionals	First level, London Chamber of Commerce and Industry ("LCCI") Group Certificate	5
	Second level, LCCI Group Certificate	10
	Third level, LCCI Group Certificate	20
	Preliminary examination of Association of Accounting Technicians ("AAT")	30
	Intermediate examination of AAT	40
	Final examination of AAT	50
6. Engineers and related professionals	Part I Professional Examination	10
	Part II Professional Examination	20
	Practical training, Stage 1	30
	Practical training, Stage 2	40
	Membership or fellowship of professional institution	50
7. Architects, planners and surveyors	Part I Professional Examination	10
	Part II Professional Examination	20
	Part III Professional Examination	35
	Membership or fellowship of professional institution	50
8. Engineering associate professionals	Engineering certificate or diploma	10
	Polytechnic higher certificate	20
	Polytechnic higher diploma	35
	Polytechnic endorsement certificate	50
9. Information science professionals	Diploma or certificate	20

Specified occupational group	Qualification	Points
	Higher or advanced diploma or certificate or associate membership of professional institution	40
	Bachelor degree in information science	45
	Membership or fellowship of professional institution	50
10. News editors and journalists	A-level in Chinese or English	10
	Certificate or diploma other than in journalism or communications	20
	Certificate or diploma in journalism or communications	30
	Bachelor degree other than in journalism or communications	45
	Bachelor degree in journalism or communications	50
11. Medical doctors	Medical graduate provisionally registered with Medical Council of Hong Kong	10
	Practising certificate issued by Medical Council of Hong Kong	15
	Licentiate of Medical Council of Hong Kong	25
	Registered medical practitioner	50
12. Physical and life science professionals	Post-secondary certificate or diploma	35
	Bachelor degree	45
	Membership or fellowship of professional institution	50

Specified occupational group	Qualification	Points
13. Nurses and midwives	Certificate of enrolment with Nursing Board of Hong Kong or Certificate of registration with Midwives Board of Hong Kong	30
	Certificate of registration with Nursing Board of Hong Kong	50
14. Other medical professionals (except nurses and midwives)	Professions registerable under the Dentists Registration Ordinance (Chapter 156 of the Laws of Hong Kong) or the Pharmacy and Poisons Ordinance (Chapter 138 of the Laws of Hong Kong)	
	Certificate or Diploma	30
	Bachelor degree	40
	Registered as medical professional	50
	Professions not registerable under any Hong Kong Ordinance	
	Certificate	30
	Diploma	40
	Bachelor degree	50
15. Health associate professionals (except nurses and midwices)	Matriculation	10
	Certificate or diploma (other than a professional diploma)	30
	Professional diploma	50
16. Legal professionals	Bachelor degree in law	10
	Post-graduate certificate in law	20
	Completion of articles or pupillage	35
	Registered lawyer	50

Specified occupational group	Qualification	Points
17. Legal associate professionals	Hong Kong Certificate of Education Examination	10
	Matriculation	25
	Polytechnic higher certificate or diploma	50
18. Teaching professionals (post-secondary)	Teacher certificate	10
	Bachelor degree	20
	Post-graduate diploma	25
	Post-graduate degree (other than by research)	30
	Post-graduate degree by research (other than Ph.D)	40
	Ph.D	50
19. Educational administrators	Teacher certificate	20
	Post-secondary certificate or diploma	35
	Associate membership of professional institution	40
	Bachelor degree or membership or fellowship of professional institution	50
20. Other teaching personnel	Teacher's permit	5
	Qualified kindergarten teacher	10
	Diploma or certificate from polytechnic or technical institute	25
	Completion of In-Service Training Course for Teachers	30
	Teacher certificate	35

Specified occupational group	Qualification	Points
	Bachelor of Education degree obtained after 1 or 2 years full-time study	40
	Bachelor degree (other than Bachelor of Education)	45
	Bachelor degree (other than Bachelor of Education) together with teacher certificate; or completion of Bachelor of Education degree obtained after 3 or 4 years full-time study	50

Explanatory Note

(This note is not part of the Order)

Section 1(1) of the British Nationality (Hong Kong) Act 1990 provides that the Secretary of State shall register as British citizens up to 50,000 persons recommended to him for that purpose by the Governor of Hong Kong under a scheme or schemes made and approved in accordance with Schedule 1 to that Act. Paragraph 1 of that Schedule provides that effect shall be given to any such scheme by an Order in Council setting out the terms of the scheme. Paragraph 2(a) of the Schedule provides that the scheme set out in the Order in Council shall, in the case of the first Order to be made, be a scheme submitted by the Governor with such modifications (if any) as the Secretary of State may think necessary or expedient.

This Order is the first to be made under the Act and gives effect in the Schedule thereto, without modifications, to a scheme submitted by the Governor. The scheme provides that the Governor may make recommendations in respect of persons falling within four classes within a quota prescribed by the scheme. Those classes (with the respective quotas in brackets) are the general occupational class (36,200), the disciplined services class (7,000), the sensitive service class (6,300) and the entrepreneurs class (500).

Part II of the scheme makes provision for the general occupational class and provides for applicants to be recommended according to the number of points allocated to them within the quota prescribed by the scheme for the particular occupation or occupational group in which they apply. Under Part II points are allocated to an applicant for age, experience, education and training, special circumstances, proficiency in the English language, connections with the United Kingdom and public and community service.

Part III provides for the disciplined services class and makes provision for the points scheme set out in Part II to apply to applicants in the disciplined services with modifications. It also provides for the Governor to recommend applicants in the sensitive service class (in respect of the applicant's service in the interests of the Crown or other activities of a sensitive nature) and in the entrepreneurs class if the Governor considers that the applicant has made a significant contribution to the economy of Hong Kong.

Part IV makes provision for supplemental matters and, in particular, prevents any applicant who is concerned with the implementation of the scheme from dealing with any matter concerned with, or arising from, his own application or any application in which he has a personal interest.

(1) 1990 c. 34.
(2) 1981 c. 61.
(3) S.I. 1986/948.

《香港（英國國籍）（修訂）令 1993》

BRITISH NATIONALITY

The Hong Kong (British Nationality) (Amendment) Order 1993

Made	20th July 1993
Coming into force	21st July 1993

At the Court at Buckingham Palace, the 20th day of July 1993

Present,

The Queen's Most Excellent Majesty in Council

Whereas a draft of this Order has been laid before Parliament and has been approved by a resolution of each House of Parliament:

Now, therefore, Her Majesty, in pursuance of paragraph 2 of the Schedule to the Hong Kong Act 1985(1) is pleased, by and with the advice of Her Privy Council, to order, and it is hereby ordered, as follows:

1. —(1) This Order may be cited as the Hong Kong (British Nationality) (Amend-ment) Order 1993 and shall come into force on the day after the day on which it is made.

(2) This Order extends to Northern Ireland.

(3) This Order extends to the Channel Islands and the Isle of Man and to all dependent territories.

(4) Section 50 of the British Nationality Act 1981(2) (interpretation) shall apply to the interpretation of this Order as it applies to the interpretation of that Act.

2. The Hong Kong (British Nationality) Order 1986(3) shall be amended as follows–

(a) in article 4(2) after the words "would not be such a citizen," shall be inserted the words "and who applies on or before the relevant date"; and

(b) after article 4(3) there shall be added–

"(4) An application for registration under paragraph (2) above made after the relevant date may be accepted if the applicant shows that there are special circumstances which justify his being so registered.

(5) Where any person is registered (or naturalised) as a British Dependent Territories citizen by virtue (wholly or partly) of his having a connection with Hong Kong, after, or less than three months before, the relevant date, the Secretary of State shall register him as a British National (Overseas) if he applies within three months after the date of his registration (or naturalisation) as a British Dependent Territories citizen.

(6) In this article "the relevant date" in relation to a person whose year of birth falls within one of the entries in column 1 of the Second Schedule to this Order, means the date shown in the corresponding entry in column 2.".

3. Section 42 of the British Nationality Act 1981 shall be amended so as to add, after subsection (5)–

"(6) A person who applies for registration or naturalisation as a British Dependent Territories citizen under any provision of this Act by virtue (wholly or partly) of his having a connection with Hong Kong, may not be naturalised or registered, as the case may be, unless he makes his application on or before 31st March 1996.".

4.—(1) The Schedule to the Hong Kong (British Nationality) Order 1986 shall become the first Schedule to that Order and, as a consequence, in article 8 for the words "the Schedule" there shall be substituted the words "the first Schedule".

(2) After the first Schedule to that Order there shall be added the Schedule set out in the Schedule to this Order.

N. H. Nicholls
Clerk of the Privy Council

SCHEDULE SECOND SCHEDULE

Timetable for the receipt of applications for the registration of British Dependent Territories citizens as British Nationals (Overseas).

Column 1	Column 2
Year of birth of British Dependent Territories citizen	Final date for receipt of applications
1967 to 1971	30th October 1993
1962 to 1966	31st March 1994
1957 to 1961	31st August 1994
1947 to 1956	28th February 1995
Prior to 1947	30th June 1995
1972 to 1976	31st October 1995
1977 to 1981	30th March 1996
1982 to 1986	29th June 1996
1987 to 1991	30th September 1996
1992 to 1995	31st December 1996
1996	31st March 1997
1997	30th September 1997

Explanatory Note

(This note is not part of the Order)

This Order makes provision with regard to the British nationality status of persons who are British Dependent Territories citizens by virtue of a connection with Hong Kong and with regard to persons who wish to be registered as such citizens. This Order amends the Hong Kong (British Nationality) Order 1986 and the British Nationality Act 1981.

Article 2 amends article 4 of the 1986 Order and makes provision for the operation of a series of dates, up until 30th September 1997, before which British Dependent Territories citizens seeking the status of British National (Overseas) must apply for it. The relevant date for each applicant depends on the year of his birth and is listed in the Schedule, which becomes the Second Schedule to the 1986 Order.

Article 3 amends section 42 of the 1981 Act so as to provide that a person seeking registration or naturalisation as a British Dependent Territories citizen by virtue of his having a connection with Hong Kong, must make his application on or before 31st March 1996.

(1) 1985 c. 15.

(2) 1981 c. 61; section 50 was amended by the Hong Kong (British Nationality) Order 1986, article 7(8) (S.I. 1986/948).

(3) S.I. 1986/948.

《英國海外領土法 2002》

British Overseas Territories Act 2002

2002 CHAPTER 8

An Act to make provision about the name "British overseas territories" and British citizenship so far as relating to the British overseas territories.

[26th February 2002]

Be it enacted by the Queen's most Excellent Majesty, by and with the advice and consent of the Lords Spiritual and Temporal, and Commons, in this present Parliament assembled, and by the authority of the same, as follows:—

1. British overseas territories

This section has no associated Explanatory Notes

(1) As the territories mentioned in Schedule 6 to the British Nationality Act 1981 (c. 61) are now known as "British overseas territories"—

(a) in section 50(1) of that Act (definitions), at the appropriate place insert—

""British overseas territory" means a territory mentioned in Schedule 6;",

(b) for "dependent territory" (or "dependent territories"), wherever occurring in that Act, substitute " British overseas territory "(or " British overseas territories "), and

(c) in the heading to that Schedule, for "British Dependent

Territories" substitute " British Overseas Territories ".

(2) In any other enactment passed or made before the commencement of this section (including an enactment comprised in subordinate legislation), any reference to a dependent territory within the meaning of the British Nationality Act 1981 shall be read as a reference to a British overseas territory.

(3) In the Interpretation Act 1978 (c. 30), at the appropriate place in Schedule 1 (list of definitions) insert—

2. ""British overseas territory" has the same meaning as in the British Nationality Act 1981;".

(1) Pursuant to section 1, British Dependent Territories citizenship is renamed "British overseas territories citizenship"; and a person having that citizenship is a "British overseas territories citizen".

(2) Accordingly, in the British Nationality Act 1981 (c. 61)—

(a) for "British Dependent Territories citizenship", wherever occurring, substitute " British overseas territories citizenship ", and

(b) for "British Dependent Territories citizen" (or "British Dependent Territories citizens"), wherever occurring, substitute " British overseas territories citizen "(or " British overseas territories citizens").

(3) In any other enactment passed or made before the commencement of this section (including an enactment comprised in subordinate legislation), any reference to British Dependent Territories citizenship, or a British Dependent Territories citizen, shall be read as a reference to British overseas territories citizenship, or a British overseas territories citizen.

3. Conferral on British overseas territories citizens

(1) Any person who, immediately before the commencement of this section, is a British overseas territories citizen shall, on the commencement of this section, become a British citizen.

(2) Subsection (1) does not apply to a person who is a British

overseas territories citizen by virtue only of a connection with the Sovereign Base Areas of Akrotiri and Dhekelia.

(3) A person who is a British citizen by virtue of this section is a British citizen by descent for the purposes of the British Nationality Act 1981 if, and only if—

(a) he was a British overseas territories citizen by descent immediately before the commencement of this section, and

(b) if at that time he was a British citizen as well as a British overseas territories citizen, he was a British citizen by descent.

4. Acquisition by British overseas territories citizens by registration

After section 4 of the British Nationality Act 1981 insert—

"4A Acquisition by registration: further provision for British overseas territories citizens

(1) If an application is made to register as a British citizen a person who is a British overseas territories citizen, the Secretary of State may if he thinks fit cause the person to be so registered.

(2) Subsection (1) does not apply in the case of a British overseas territories citizen who—

(a) is such a citizen by virtue only of a connection with the Sovereign Base Areas of Akrotiri and Dhekelia; or

(b) has ceased to be a British citizen as a result of a declaration of renunciation."

5. Acquisition by reference to the British overseas territories.

Schedule 1 (which makes provision about the acquisition of British citizenship by reference to the British overseas territories) has effect.

6. The Ilois: citizenship

(1) A person shall become a British citizen on the commencement of this section if—

(a) he was born on or after 26 April 1969 and before 1 January

1983,

(b) he was born to a woman who at the time was a citizen of the United Kingdom and Colonies by virtue of her birth in the British Indian Ocean Territory, and

(c) immediately before the commencement of this section he was neither a British citizen nor a British overseas territories citizen.

(2) A person who is a British citizen by virtue of subsection (1) is a British citizen by descent for the purposes of the British Nationality Act 1981 (c. 61).

(3) A person shall become a British overseas territories citizen on the commencement of this section if—

(a) subsection (1)(a) and (b) apply in relation to him, and

(b) immediately before the commencement of this section he was not a British overseas territories citizen.

(4) A person who is a British overseas territories citizen by virtue of subsection (3) is such a citizen by descent for the purposes of the British Nationality Act 1981.

7. Repeals

The enactments mentioned in Schedule 2 (which include some which are spent or effectively superseded) are repealed to the extent specified there.

8. Short title, commencement and extent

(1) This Act may be cited as the British Overseas Territories Act 2002.

(2) The following provisions of this Act are to come into force on such day as the Secretary of State may by order made by statutory instrument appoint—

(a) sections 3 to 5 and Schedule 1,

(b) section 6, and

(c) section 7 and Schedule 2, so far as relating to the British Nationality (Falkland Islands) Act 1983 (c. 6).

(3) An order under subsection (2) may—

(a) appoint different days for different purposes, and

(b) include such transitional provision as the Secretary of State considers expedient.

(4) This Act extends to—

(a) the United Kingdom,

(b) the Channel Islands and the Isle of Man, and

(c) the British overseas territories.

入境事務處處長 對 莊豐源；
FACV 26/2000

〔**簡略案情**〕

答辯人是一名中國公民，屬未成年人士，由祖父及起訴監護人莊曜誠代表。答辯人在 1997 年 9 月 29 日於香港出生，亦即是在香港特區成立以後出生，當時，他的父母只是持雙程證來港的中國公民，在答辯人出生及以後的時間，父母任何一方都沒有在香港定居或享有居留權。答辯人聲稱他屬《基本法》第 24 條第 2 款第 1 項所指的永久性居民，並享有居留權。雖然入境事務處處長（"處長"）接納答辯人是在特區成立後於香港出生的中國公民，但否決其聲稱。處長認為香港法例第 115 章《入境條例》附表 1 第 2（a）段（"第 2（a）段"）規定 "在香港出生的中國公民若要成為永久性居民，則在其出生時或其後任何時間，其父母的任何一方必須已在香港定居或已享有香港居留權。"（註）而按《基本法》第 24 條第 2 款第 1 項的正確解釋，該條款並不賦予非法入境、逾期居留或在香港臨時居留的人在香港所生的中國公民居留權。故此，處長認為第 2（a）段與《基本法》相符。又因答辯人的父母在其出生時或其後任何時間，均沒有在香港定居或享有香港居留權，所以他不符《基本法》第 24 條第 2 款第 1 項的規定。

但原審法官批准答辯人司法覆核的申請，並裁定第 2（a）

段有關父母的規定與《基本法》第 24 條第 2 款第 1 項相抵觸，同時宣告答辯人為香港特區的永久性居民，享有香港特區居留權。上訴法庭維持原審法官的命令，駁回處長的上訴。

吳嘉玲、吳丹丹 對 入境事務處處長；
FACV 16/1998

〔簡略案情〕

　　吳嘉玲小姐及吳丹丹小姐兩人是姊妹，是內地出生的中國籍人士。她倆分別於 1987 年及 1989 年出生，當時她們的父親已是在香港通常居住連續七年以上的中國公民。他在 1976 年來港，而兩名申請人則於 1997 年 7 月 1 日沒有通過入境管制站而進入本港。1997 年 7 月 4 日她們向入境處報到，堅稱根據《基本法》第 24（2）條第三款擁有居留權，但她們的權利未獲入境處處長承認。入境處將她們拘捕，其後批准他們領取擔保書外出。

　　原訟庭和上訴庭皆認為根據《基本法》第 22（4）條制定的《入境（修訂）（第 3 號）條例》是合法和有效的，因此，他們必須獲得以單程證形式簽發的出境批准，才可享有居留權。對此，申請人上訴至終審法院。

談雅然、陳偉華 對 入境事務處處長；
FACV 21/2000

〔簡略案情〕

　　上訴人談雅然、陳偉華及謝曉怡（"上訴人"）均屬內地出生未成年的中國公民。他們根據內地法律被領養，而且，在他們被領養時，或事實上在他們出生時，領養父母雙方或一方已成為香港永久性居民。與訟各方同意各上訴人乃根據內地法律所接受的領養，屬香港法例第 290 章《領養條例》第 17 條所述的海外領養，因此，該等領養與該條例下的有效領養令具相同效力，即：

　　…… 幼年人真正父母所具有的關於幼年人的權利及義務均告終絕，領養子女在與領養人的關係中，須完全處於屬領養人在婚姻中所生的子女的地位 …… 其與真正父母之間的家庭關係將完全及永久終止；就所有事項而言，領養父母的地位須猶如真正父母一樣。

　　上訴人堅稱他們屬第 24 條第 2 款第（3）項所指的永久性居民，並享有居留權。處長對此提出爭議。案件初審時原訟法庭法官判決上訴人勝訴，入境事務處處長提出上訴。上訴法庭裁定入境事務處處長上訴得直。

Gutierrez Josephine B. 對 人事登記處處長及人事登記審裁處；
HCAL 136/2010

〔簡略案情〕

　　申請人為菲律賓國籍母子兩人。母親從 1991 年開始一直被批准在香港做家庭傭工，期間一共轉換過八個僱主，並且於 1996 年在香港跟一位美國人誕下其第五名兒子，即現在的兒子申請人，但她跟該男子已經失去聯繫。在 2006 年 12 月，兩位申請人根據《入境條例》附表一、第 2（f）條要求入境處核實他們的永久居民身份但被拒。而他們於 2008 年向人事登記處申請永久居民身份證的要求亦不被接納，他們遂向人事登記審裁處提出上訴。可是，審裁處最後認定他們並不能證明他們以香港作為永久居住地，而拒絕他們的上訴。申請人遂向原訟庭提起司法覆核申請，要求推翻人事登記處和人事登記審裁處的決定。母親認為審裁處忽略了她已經在香港生活了 19 年，完全融入了本地的環境，在菲律賓已經沒有家庭，大部份兒女都在香港生活。而且，她所有資產也在香港，社交圈子亦主要是本地的教會並打算在香港終老，因此她已經把香港作為永久居住地。至於兒子，由出生開始 15 年裏一直以香港為家，他的生活建立在香港也紮根在香港，而這個也是他唯一的家。

Maura Juliet A. Raquiza 對 入境事務處處長；

CACV 272/2006

〔簡略案情〕

申請人是菲律賓人，1988 年 8 月 26 日開始在港從事家庭傭工，其逗留許可被多次延長至 1992 年 2 月 27 日。因其僱傭合約於 1992 年 1 月 7 日被終止，她只被批准以遊客身份逗留至同年 1 月 28 日。其間，她於 1 月 23 日簽了新的僱傭合約，並且於 26 日離港回菲等待新合約的處理。她在 1992 年 6 月返港工作，後因續約而獲准延長逗留至 1997 年 7 月 15 日。在 1996 年 10 月 15 日，申請人與一香港永久性居民結婚。由 1997 年 4 月 14 日起她便以家屬身份在香港居住。不幸地，其丈夫於 1997 年 12 月搬離他們的居所並於 1999 年 1 月申請離婚。然而，申請人與其丈夫似乎於同年 5 月 達成了協定，其丈夫會取消離婚申請並承擔延續申請人家屬簽證的申請。事實上，申請人的家屬簽證最後被延至 2003 年 3 月 15 日。在該婚姻破裂後，申請人於 2001 年 5 月 16 日基於已經以家屬簽證在港居留 3 年以上為由，申請無條件逗留。因為申請人沒有應處長的要求出席會面，該申請於翌年 8 月被認定為放棄。申請人在其 逗留許可屆滿前（即 2003 年 3 月 15 日前），經一家律師所幫助，以不同理由再作出申請。首先，她以其丈夫作承擔人，其後她又以她本人作承擔人提出申請。正當這些申請被覆核期間,申請人丈夫又表示願意作為該申請的承擔人。因此,申請人與其丈夫於 2003 年 6 月 9 日被入境處分別接見。會談中申請人丈夫表達了與申請人復合的意願,同時亦願意繼續支持申請人在香港居住。可是,申請人於同日則表示她想離婚和不再需要家屬簽證。申請人確認入境處主任曾向她指出如果她離婚,她將需要離開香港,然而,申請人表示她只希望能延長一個月時間好讓她能處理強積金和離婚事宜。最後,按照她的意願,她被批准延長逗留至同年 7 月 9 日。往後的延期申請一律被處方拒絕。

陳錦雅及其他 80 人 對 入境事務處處長；
FACV 13/1998

〔簡略案情〕

　　上訴人由其父親作為監護人代表訴訟，並在本案中代表其餘 80 位情況跟她類同的訴訟人，其中有 12 位是成年人士。各上訴人的基本情況大致相同，即他們都是在內地出生的中國公民，在他們出生時其父母都不是香港的永久性居民，但是在此之後，其父母中至少一方在香港連續居住 7 年以上獲得了永久性居民的身份。這些上訴人部份持雙程證入境，部份為非法入境者。面對入境事務處處長的遣返令，他們同時以《基本法》第 24 條（2）第 2 和第 3 款來反對，並申請作為香港永久性居民，繼續留在香港。入境事務處認為依據《人民入境（修訂）（第 2 號）條例》中的相關規定，各原告並不符合作為香港永久性居民的條件，因為他們父母在他們出生時並未獲得香港永久性居民的身份。所以，法庭面對的問題是《基本法》第 24 條（2）第 3 款只適用於該子女出生時其中一方父母已經是香港永久居民。

作者簡介

　　李浩然，清華大學憲法學博士。自 2003 年起一直從事「一國兩制」及《基本法》的研究。曾在香港出版《香港基本法起草過程概覽》（全三冊）（2012 年）、《香港基本法案例彙編》（1997-2010）（第一條至第四十二條）（合著）（2013 年）、《行政長官產生辦法考——基本法第 45 條起草過程概覽》（2015 年）、《以法達治》（2015 年）、《香港基本法案例彙編（1997-2010）（第四十三條至第一百六十條）（合著）（2019 年）、《「一國兩制」下的香港法治和管治研究》（2019 年）及《國安法　廿三條　安全與自由？——國家安全法之立法及比較研究》（合著）（2020 年）。

　　李博士因基本法研究和教育工作成就突出，於 2016 年獲香港特區政府頒授榮譽勳章（MH）、2017 年獲選為香港十大傑出青年、2019 年獲香港特區政府頒授太平紳士（JP）。

　　尹國華，現為執業大律師，師從戴啟思、梁家傑等資深大律師。香港大學物理系學士，1989 年放棄博士生獎學金，於港大轉讀法律；期間曾取得獎學金赴劍橋大學進修。2002 年於北京清華大學修讀法律。近年偶於香港大學專業進修學院教授法律課程。著有《香港基本法案例彙編》（1997-2010）（第一條至第四十二條）（合著）（2013 年）及《香港基本法案例彙編 (1997-2010)（第四十三條至第一百六十條））（合著）（2019 年）及《國安法　廿三條　安全與自由？——國家安全法之立法及比較研究》（合著）（2020 年）。